The Wampanoag

The People of the First Light

by Janet Riehecky

Bridgestone Books

an imprint of Capstone Press
Mankato, Minnesota

Bridgestone Books are published by Capstone Press
151 Good Counsel Drive • P.O. Box 669 • Mankato, Minnesota 56002
http://www.capstone-press.com

Printed in the United States of America

Library of Congress Cataloging-in-Publication Data
Riehecky, Janet, 1953–
The Wampanoag: the people of the first light / by Janet Riehecky.
p. cm.—(American Indian nations)
Summary: An introduction to the history, social structure, customs, beliefs, ceremonies, and day-to-day life of the Wampanoag Indians who had been living in the southern New England area for thousands of years before the arrival of English settlers in 1620.
Includes bibliographical references and index.
ISBN 0-7368-1568-6 (hardcover)
1. Wampanoag Indians—Juvenile literature. [1. Wampanoag Indians. 2. Indians of North America—New England.] I. Title. II. Series: American Indian nations series.
E99.W2.R54 2003
974.4004'973—dc21 2002010326

Editorial Credits

Bradley P. Hoehn, editor; Christopher Harbo, editor; Kia Adams, designer and illustrator; Wanda Winch, photo researcher; Karen Risch, product planning editor

Photo Credits

Ben Klaffke, cover (main), 14–15; Cape Cod Times, 45; Cape Cod Times/Ron Schloerb, cover (inset); Cape Cod Times/Kevin Mingora, 32, 37; Cape Cod Times/Matt Suess, 43; Capstone Press/Gary Sundermeyer, 17; Corbis/Rose Hartman, 18; Corbis/Bettman, 24–25; The Granger Collection, 22–23; Kathy Sharp Frisbee, 4, 38; Marilyn "Angel" Wynn, 44; Mary Lopez, 35, 41; National Park Service–Colonial National Historic Park, 20–21; North Wind Picture Archives, 27, 31; Photo Network/Michael Philip Manheim, 7; Stock Montage, Inc., 29; Tara Prindle, 8, 12

Capstone Press thanks the Education Department of the Wampanoag Tribe of Gay Head (Aquinnah) in Aquinnah, Massachusetts for their help in reading and responding to this book.

1 2 3 4 5 6 08 07 06 05 04 03

Table of Contents

1 Who Are the Wampanoag? 5
2 Traditional Life 9
3 Pilgrims Bring Change 21
4 Wampanoag Today. 33
5 Sharing the Traditions. 39

Features

Map: Wampanoag Lands. 11
Recipe: Cranberry Shortcake 17
Timeline. 44
Glossary. 46
Internet Sites 46
Places to Write and Visit. 47
For Further Reading. 47
Index 48

The Wampanoag live in southeastern Massachusetts and the islands off the Massachusetts coast.

Chapter One

Who Are the Wampanoag?

The people of the Wampanoag (wam-puh-NO-ag) Indian Nation have lived in the southern New England area for thousands of years. The name Wampanoag means "People of the First Light." Before 1600, about 16,000 Wampanoag lived in more than 60 villages. They lived in what is now southeastern Massachusetts and eastern Rhode Island. They also lived on the islands off the coast of Massachusetts. The Wampanoag still live in that area today.

Plymouth

In the early 1600s, disease killed thousands of American Indians, including more than half of the Wampanoag. Historians think American Indians caught smallpox and other diseases from traders. Often whole villages died.

The Wampanoag were the first American Indians to meet the Pilgrims. In 1620, the Pilgrims landed in southeastern Massachusetts. They built the town of Plymouth on the site of the deserted village of Patuxet. The Wampanoag helped the Pilgrims survive their second winter in North America.

Most Wampanoag never left their ancestal homelands in Massachusetts. Over the centuries, they worked to preserve their traditions, and their numbers slowly grew. By the early 1900s, several thousand Wampanoag lived in Massachusetts.

Several Wampanoag tribes continue to live in Massachusetts today. They are the Aquinnah, Chappaquiddick, Herring Pond, Mashpee, and Nemasket tribes. A Wampanoag community also exists at Assonet. Each Wampanoag tribe has its own government, including a chief, medicine man, and council. Each tribe elects a council to lead the community.

The Wampanoag also live throughout the United States and Canada. About 2,300 people identified themselves as Wampanoag in the 2000 U.S. Census. The Wampanoag estimate there are about 4,000 tribal members today.

Today, many of the Wampanoag people live like other North Americans. Some continue the long tradition of farming and fishing. Others work at jobs in a variety of fields. Wampanoag scholars helped plan and build the Wampanoag Indian Program at Plimoth Plantation, a model of the colony of Plymouth. Wampanoag people work at Plimoth Plantation, re-creating their life in the 1600s. They take pride in teaching others how their ancestors lived.

Visitors to Plimoth Plantation can learn how the Wampanoag lived during the 1600s.

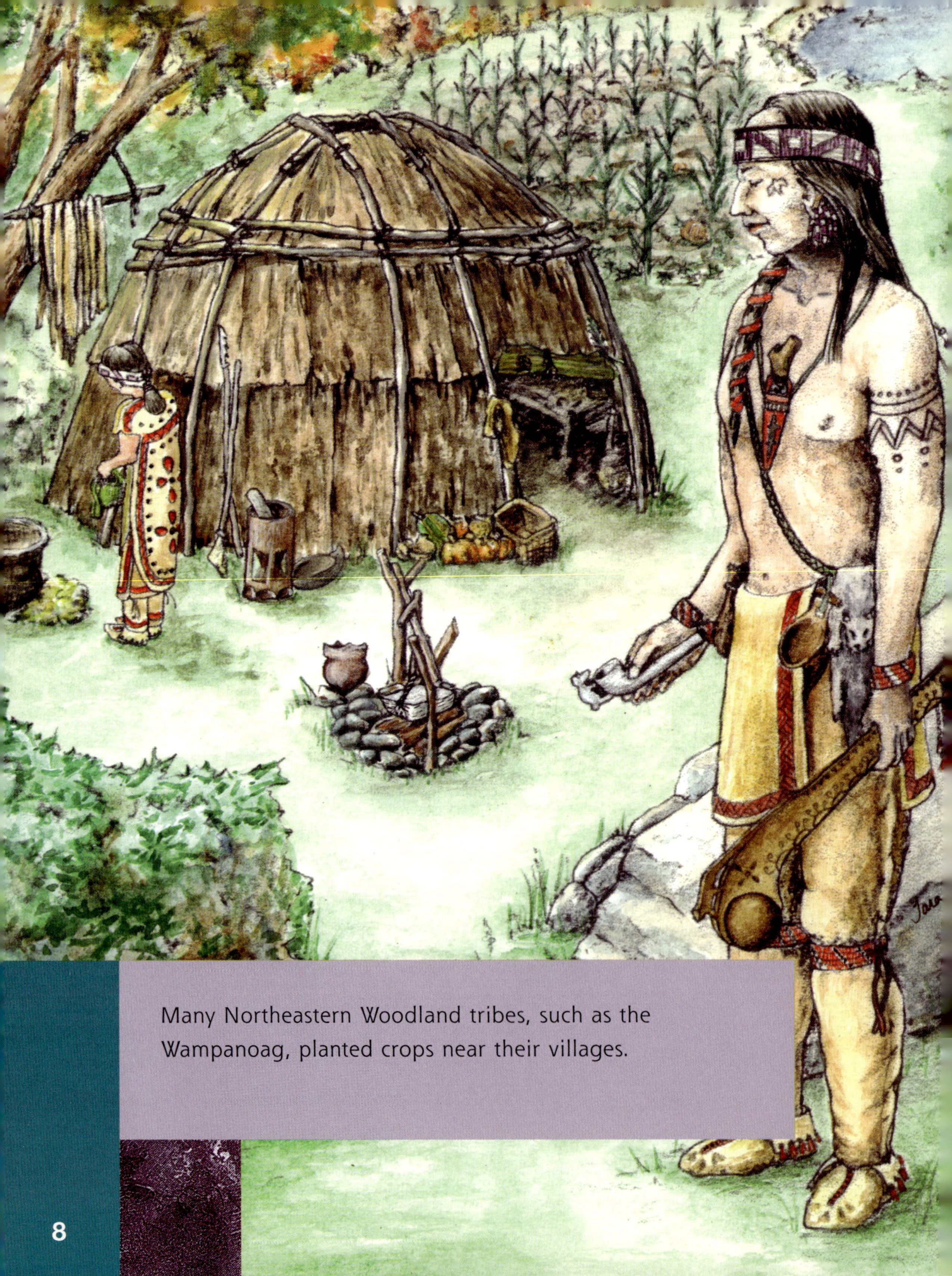

Many Northeastern Woodland tribes, such as the Wampanoag, planted crops near their villages.

Chapter Two

Traditional Life

Most Wampanoag, like many Northeastern Woodland tribes, were farmers before Europeans arrived. In the spring, Wampanoag lived in villages set up near the coast. They chose areas that were easy to farm. They often returned yearly to the same site. Everyone helped clear the land.

After the harvest, the Wampanoag moved inland to a winter settlement. They chose easily defendable sites near good sources of water.

Family and Community

The heart of the Wampanoag Nation was, and still is, the family. Everyone who lived in the Wampanoag villages had an important role to play in helping the people survive. Parents, grandparents, and other family members taught children the skills they needed. Elders of the Wampanoag were as important to the community then as they are now. They cared for the children and taught them about the history and traditions of the Wampanoag.

Children did have time to play. They also learned how to do jobs they would do when they grew older. The young girls spent time with the women learning how to gather wild herbs, roots, and other foods. They learned when and how to plant crops. The women also taught girls about cooking, sewing, weaving baskets and mats, and making clay pots. The young boys learned to hunt and make tools such as knives and arrows. They also learned about fishing and building boats and homes.

The Wampanoag women planted a variety of crops, including corn, beans, pumpkins, sunflowers, squash, and tobacco. Women gathered wild berries, nuts, and herbs. During the summer, women and children cared for the crops

Wampanoag Lands Past and Present

Women and girls in Northeastern Woodland tribes, such as the Wampanoag, made baskets, mats, and pots.

by pulling weeds. The children kept mice, crows, and other animals from eating the seeds and plants.

Wampanoag men did the fishing and hunting. Men used boats to fish for cod, sturgeon, salmon, and herring. They hunted seals, porpoises, turtles, and even whales. In the woodlands, they hunted for deer, bear, and other animals.

Wampanoag did not work all the time. During the summer, they sometimes left their villages for short trips to oyster beds, waterfalls, or other villages. Meetings between villages often included contests of strength and endurance.

Hospitality was one of the most important family values of the Wampanoag. Villagers greeted travelers kindly. The Wampanoag offered travelers food and shelter. They took pride in giving whatever they had.

Housing

Wampanoag homes were called wetu (WEE-too). To make a wetu, the Wampanoag set poles made from cedar saplings into the ground. They bent the poles over and covered them with cattail reeds or bark. A wetu was either circular or oval. Most wetu were about 20 to 30 feet (6 to 9 meters) around. Each family had its own house.

If families shared a wetu, the house was larger with several places inside for fire pits. These homes were called neesquttow. A neesquttow was similar to a wetu only larger. A neesquttow was about 80 feet (24 meters) long by 20 feet (6 meters) wide. An opening covered by an animal skin served as the door. A hole in the roof allowed smoke from fire pits to escape. Extended families of grandparents, aunts, uncles, cousins, and others usually lived together.

The Wampanoag covered their wetu and neesquttow with different material for warm and cold seasons. During the summer, wetu and neesquttow were covered with mats made of cattail reeds. The light mats kept their homes cool in the summer. During the winter, homes were covered with tree bark and other material. The bark helped keep the heat inside the wetu and neesquttow.

Hunting

Hunting animals was important to the Wampanoag people. During the winter, the men hunted deer, bear, raccoon, beaver, rabbit, and other animals. They studied each animal's behavior to learn how best to hunt it. They learned to imitate bird sounds to hunt geese, ducks, turkeys, or quails.

Large families often lived in neesquttow. These large homes usually had several places for fire pits.

The villagers used nearly every animal part. Women dried and stored leftover meat. Women made clothing from the furs, and men made tools from the bones.

Accepted boundaries existed among different Indian nations. But within a nation's boundaries, land belonged to all of the people. Families grew crops on plots of land. Everyone used the forests to gather firewood or harvest nuts and berries. The streams and lakes were open to all for fishing. Hunting grounds were open for all hunters.

Spirituality

Wampanoag people believed that all things deserved respect. Traditionally, they believed in a creator. The Wampanoag believed that the Creator's spirit was present in everything, including animals, plants, water, and rocks.

The Wampanoag people always showed their appreciation for the generosity of the Creator. They gave thanks each day in many ways. Wampanoag ceremonies were elaborate. Villagers decorated their bodies with beads, feathers, and other ornaments. They offered prayer by dancing, chanting, and drumming.

Cranberry Shortcake

Cranberries are commonly grown in Massachussetts and other northeastern states. Each year, on the second Tuesday in October, the Aquinnah Wampanoag celebrate Cranberry Day. Cranberry shortcake is a common dessert served on Cranberry Day and other holidays. This recipe has been adapted from a recipe by Helen Attaquin of the Aquinnah Wampanoag.

Ingredients

2 cups (480 mL) fresh cranberries
1 cup (240 mL) sugar
3 tablespoons (45 mL) orange juice
1 cup (240 mL) diced oranges (about 2 medium oranges)
4 individual shortcakes
aerosol-style whipped cream

Equipment

dry-ingredient measuring cups
colander
saucepan
measuring spoons
large spoon

What You Do

1. Put cranberries in a colander. Rinse well with cold water and allow to drain.
2. Combine cranberries, sugar, and orange juice in a saucepan. Bring to a boil.
3. Add diced oranges and bring to a boil again. Reduce heat and simmer 10 minutes.
4. Remove saucepan from heat and allow contents to cool.
5. Spoon cranberry mixture onto shortcakes.
6. Top with small amounts of whipped cream.

Makes 4 servings

Moshup

The Wampanoag tell the legend of Moshup, a giant who lived thousands of years ago. Many versions of the story are told. This version was adapted from "Wampanoag Way: An Aquinnah Cultural Trail" by the Aquinnah Wampanoag.

In the olden times, a kind giant named Moshup roamed the land. One day, Moshup was making his way across the mainland to the headlands of the Aquinnah Cliffs. Tired from his journey, Moshup dragged his foot heavily, leaving a deep track in the mud. At first, only a thin thread of water trickled in the track. But slowly, the ocean's force of wind and tides broadened and deepened the opening. An island named Noepe was created.

At that time, whales swam close to the shores of Noepe. They were not afraid of being chased and caught. From near the entrance to his den on the Aquinnah Cliffs, Moshup would wade into the ocean. He would pick up a whale and throw it against the cliffs to kill it. Then he would cook the whale over the fire that always burned. The blood from these whales stained the clay banks of the cliffs dark red. The coals of Moshup's fire, whale bones, and shark's teeth are still found today in the cliffs. They are left over from Moshup's table.

The Aquinnah Cliffs are a sacred place to the Aquinnah Wampanoag. They tell the stories of one hundred million years of history.

Government

Each village in the Wampanoag Nation had its own sachem. Sachems made decisions for the village. They had many responsibilities and guarded the welfare of their people. People often came to sachems to settle disagreements. Widows, orphans, and the elderly looked to sachems to provide food and protection.

Sachems managed trade with other villages. People showed their gratitude by giving gifts of food to the sachems. The sachem worked with the advice of a council of elders and other respected people.

The villagers discussed problems until agreements were reached and decisions could be made. Public opinion prevented most villagers from breaking the customs and traditions of the village. The role of sachem usually passed from father to son, sometimes to a daughter, but always remained in the family.

Many American Indian nations, including the Wampanoag, traded with Europeans in the 1500s.

Chapter Three

Pilgrims Bring Change

In the late 1500s, Europeans traveled to the New England area. The Europeans traded with American Indians. The metal tools Europeans offered made hunting and farming easier and more effective.

Unfortunately, Europeans did not always keep their agreements. They sometimes used force to get what they wanted. They even kidnapped Wampanoag leaders and sold them into slavery. They also exposed the Wampanoag to new diseases. Smallpox, the plague, and measles killed thousands of Wampanoag.

The Pilgrims

Until the early 1600s, the Wampanoag kept their traditions and way of life, despite the loss of so many of their people. On December 16, 1620, a small ship named the *Mayflower* landed on the coast of present-day Massachusetts. It carried pilgrims and adventurers seeking religious freedom. This time the Europeans had not come to trade. They had come to settle.

The settlers chose to live at the deserted site of Patuxet, a Wampanoag village. No one lived there because disease had killed the people. The Pilgrims named their village Plymouth.

Few Wampanoag lived near the village. Europeans had treated the Wampanoag unfairly in the past. The Wampanoag did not want to be treated unfairly again. They watched the Pilgrims and waited.

During their first winter, half of the 102 colonists died from diseases, accidents, cold, and lack of food. The remaining settlers were weak and had few survival skills. The Wampanoag could have attacked the village, but they knew these settlers were no threat.

Still, the Pilgrims had stronger weapons than the Wampanoag had. The Wampanoag hoped to get weapons to use against their enemies, the Narragansett Indians. The Narragansett were the stronger tribe after the diseases had killed so many Wampanoag. The Narragansett demanded that the Wampanoag obey and honor them. The Wampanoag decided to make a treaty with the settlers.

In the 1600s, early settlers built log cabins to help survive the long, cold northeastern winters.

First Contact

On March 16, 1621, a warrior stepped out of the woods near Plymouth. He greeted the settlers in broken English. His

Massasoit and 60 other sachems met with the Pilgrims in Plymouth on March 16, 1621.

name was Samoset. He was an Abenaki Indian. Samoset lived in what is now eastern Maine. He spoke a language very similar to the Wampanoag. Samoset had learned some English from fishermen. An English sea captain named Thomas Dermer brought him south to the Wampanoag territory. Samoset stayed with the Wampanoag for about eight months.

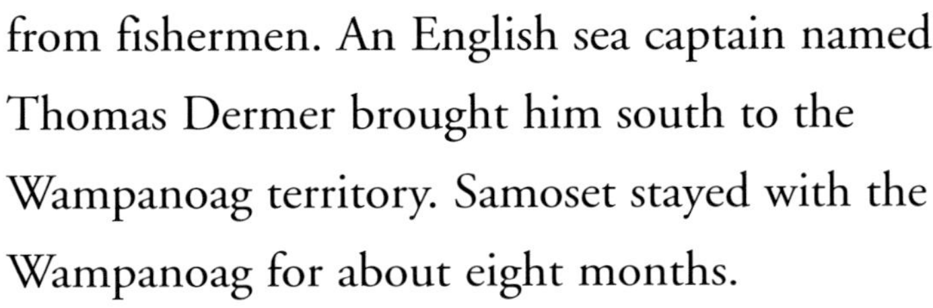

The Pilgrims were eager to learn everything they could about the native people. Samoset and the pilgrim leaders talked late into the evening. Samoset shared his information freely. In return, the Pilgrims gave him gifts and fed him with the best food available. Samoset stayed overnight. When he left, he said he would return with members of the Wampanoag tribe.

Massasoit, a sachem of the Pokanoket Wampanoag, came to Plymouth with 60 sachems. He also brought a Wampanoag named Squanto. Squanto had been from the Patuxet village.

English sailors had kidnapped Squanto when he was young and sold him into slavery. He escaped and lived with monks who taught him to speak English and helped him return to New England. When Squanto returned to Patuxet, he discovered his entire village had died from disease. He lived in other Wampanoag villages until he served as an interpreter between the Plymouth colonists and the Wampanoag.

A Peace Treaty

Massasoit negotiated a treaty with the Plymouth colonists. Each group agreed not to harm or rob the other. If either group was attacked, the other would go to its defense. Both parties agreed to leave their weapons behind when they visited each other. Each side kept this treaty during Massasoit's lifetime.

Wampanoag people helped the colonists. Squanto stayed with the colonists and taught them the skills they needed to survive. Massasoit also sent a warrior named Hobbamock to stay in Plymouth. Hobbamock served as a guide and interpreter for the colonists. Without the help of Squanto and other Wampanoag, it is unlikely that the colony would have survived.

Over the next several years, each group helped the other. The Wampanoag gave the colonists food and information. Once, when an English boy was lost, the Wampanoag found him and returned him to the village. Another time, a rival sachem attempted to overthrow Massasoit, and the colonists came to his aid. They were also able to help when Massasoit became gravely ill.

"The First Thanksgiving"

In the fall of 1621, the Plymouth colonists harvested their first crops. Squanto and other Wampanoag had given them help and good advice. The Pilgrims decided to hold a feast to give thanks. This kind of celebration was familiar to the Wampanoag. The Wampanoag had always thanked the Creator for a good harvest. The Wampanoag celebrated many thanksgivings throughout the year.

Massasoit, his family, and 90 sachems and warriors arrived at the beginning of the celebration. The colonists were worried they would not have enough food for everyone. Massasoit sent his men hunting, and they brought back five deer. The celebration lasted for three days.

Wampanoag and English Conflict

Although Massasoit stayed loyal to the treaty, the English and the Wampanoag had disagreements from time to time. Usually, the leaders were able to settle the arguments without fighting. Some disagreements were about how much land was bought or sold. Other arguments involved English pigs and horses that ruined Wampanoag cornfields. Many disagreements were about how everyone was not always following the Peace Treaty of 1621.

In 1661, Massasoit died. The number of disagreements grew quickly after his death. Without his leadership, many of the disagreements were left unsettled.

Less than one year after Massasoit's death, the English wondered if Wamsutta, his oldest son, was thinking of fighting a war against them. The English forced Wamsutta to go to Plymouth to answer their questions. After a short time in the colony, Wamsutta grew seriously ill. He died on his way home to his village.

King Philip's War

In 1662, Metacom, Massasoit's second son, became sachem of the Pokanoket Wampanoag. Metacom, who became known as King Philip, watched the changes within the Wampanoag

Years of disagreement between the English and the Wampanoag led to the King Philip's War in 1675.

territory for several years. Philip felt that the English would not listen to the Wampanoag or uphold the Peace Treaty of 1621. The English began to worry that Philip was considering war against them.

Philip traveled to Wampanoag villages and neighboring tribes to gain support for the Wampanoag. While Philip was in Rhode Island, Deputy Governor John Easton wrote a letter for him. Philip sent the letter to the English at Plymouth. In this letter, Philip said that he believed Wamsutta had been poisoned. He also said that land sales were not done fairly. He told them that pigs and horses continued to ruin Wampanoag crops.

King Philip wanted the Wampanoag to be able to defend their crops without trouble from English farmers. But he realized that the demands of the English would never stop. In 1675, he worked together with several other American Indian nations to fight the English. This conflict became known as King Philip's War.

At first King Philip won his battles. But there were Indians who turned against him and helped the English. In August 1676, King Philip was killed and many Wampanoag, along with other American Indians who supported Philip, were put in prison or sold as slaves.

After King Philip's War, life was not easy for the Wampanoag. As punishment for fighting in the war, many were sold into slavery in Bermuda, Barbados, and other Caribbean countries, where many died and some have descendants alive today.

Disease and land sales also hurt the Wampanoag. Diseases broke out in a number of villages, killing more Wampanoag. In 1763, an epidemic killed two-thirds of the people in the Wampanoag settlement at Nantucket. The sale of land made life more difficult. Villagers were forced to move into other villages or into English settlements.

In the late 1700s, the Wampanoag suffered epidemics of small pox, plague, and measles that killed thousands of people.

The Aquinnah Wampanoag have always lived on their ancestral tribal lands on Martha's Vineyard. The Wampanoag name for the island is Noepe.

Chapter Four

Wampanoag Today

The Wampanoag have preserved their own culture throughout the centuries. When needed, they adapted to the customs of non-Indians. Still, the Wampanoag have never lost their own culture. Parents and grandparents continue to teach their children Wampanoag customs and traditions. Like other U.S. students, Wampanoag children can choose to attend public or private schools.

The Wampanoag Nation

The Wampanoag Nation once was more than 60 tribal villages. Although each village had the right to make its own laws and had its own sachem and council, many of the villages decided to work together for the common good.

By the early 1900s, five Wampanoag tribes remained in Massachussetts. In 1928, several Wampanoag communities organized themselves into the Wampanoag Federation. Members of the federation have pushed for federal laws to return land and repay their people for land the government has taken.

The Wampanoag Nation is still strong today. Although each tribe maintains a separate government, just as it always has, there are issues that bring the nation together.

The Wampanoag and U.S. Legislation

Many laws passed by the United States government affect the Wampanoag. One law that brings the Wampanoag Nation together is called the Native American Graves Protection and Repatriation Act. The Wampanoag and other American Indian nations worked with the U.S. government to pass this law in 1990. The law requires museums and other places to

Each July, the Mashpee Wampanoag hold a powwow for three days. Wampanoag of all ages take part in the powwow.

Native American Graves Protection and Repatriation Act

For many years, American Indian nations have objected when scientists and collectors dig up their ancient burial grounds. Members of the Wampanoag joined a national effort to draft a law so American Indian burial grounds would be treated with more respect.

On November 16, 1990, Congress passed the Native American Graves Protection and Repatriation Act. It requires museums and individuals to return human remains and items found in graves to the families or tribes of the original owners. The act also states the conditions that must be met before a scientist can work in an American Indian graveyard. Some research is still allowed, but the scientists must get permission from the descendants before digging. Anyone who does not follow this law or tries to sell items from graves could go to jail.

Since the law was passed, thousands of skeletons have been returned to different Indian nations. The process continues to return and rebury the remains of American Indians.

return skeletal remains and items from graves to the appropriate Indian nations.

Wampanoag people also helped create the Indian Child Welfare Act of 1978. This law requires orphaned American Indian children to be placed in Indian homes. If that is not possible, the parents they are placed with must help the children learn their native culture and traditions.

In 1987, the U.S. government recognized the Aquinnah Wampanoag as an official nation. The Mashpee Wampanoag also want to be recognized as a nation. Federally recognized nations can receive federal funding and other resources.

Today, about 1,000 Aquinnah Wampanoag live in the United States. About 350 of those tribal members continue to live on Martha's Vineyard.

The Wampanoag continue to practice and preserve their traditions today.

Chapter Five

Sharing the Traditions

The Wampanoag work to preserve their traditions. In the 1950s and 1960s, Wampanoag elders worried that these traditions were being lost. Tribe members were adopting the lifestyle of the non-Indian people around them. The elders spent more time instructing Wampanoag children in the old ways. When these children grew up, they became more vocal about preserving their nation and its traditions.

Wampanoag Celebrations

The Wampanoag hold many celebrations throughout the year. The Moshup Pageant is usually held in August and is open to the public in Aquinnah. It reenacts the life of Moshup, a giant who is a major character in Wampanoag stories. Clambakes can be held at any time. Most celebrations include good food, dancing, drumming, singing, and storytelling.

The Wampanoag hold celebrations that are sometimes thought of as "thanksgivings." They mark special times in the year such as the change of seasons or harvests. The Wampanoag look at signs in nature to tell them when the celebrations are to take place.

Celebrations occur during each season. In the springtime, the Wampanoag hold a celebration of the New Year. The New Year celebration marks the return of the fish called herring, as well as the new planting season. In the summer, several celebrations take place. These harvest celebrations mark the ripening of the strawberries and the early corn harvest called the Green Corn. In the fall, celebrations are held to mark the final harvest of the planted foods and the harvest of the cranberries. In the wintertime, a celebration is held to mark the shortest day of the year and the return of the sun.

In 2002, members of several Wampanoag tribes used canoes called mishoons to travel the historical water routes of their ancesters.

Today, in addition to the thanksgiving celebrations, the Wampanoag hold two other gatherings during the year. One is called powwow and the other is called a social. A powwow is a gathering of many tribes, not just the Wampanoag.

The Mashpee usually hold a powwow for three days in early July. This celebration is open to the public. Events include traditional dancing, singing, storytelling, and contests. Booths sell traditional food and Wampanoag crafts. The dress adopted for these ceremonies is not strictly Wampanoag. Some dancers and singers have adopted some elements of powwow tradition from other tribes. At some powwows there are competitions that determine the best singers and dancers at that gathering.

A social is a much smaller gathering than a powwow. At a social, the community comes together. Socials usually mark a special occasion such as the cranberry harvest on Cranberry Day or the new spring planting. Each family brings food to share. After the meal is eaten, there is singing and dancing.

The Wampanoag also share their traditions and values at Plimoth Plantation. Plimoth Plantation is a reconstruction of the original Plymouth colony. Members of the Wampanoag Nation have helped to make sure the site is accurate. Workers in native dress demonstrate the Wampanoag way of life.

Shawl dancers compete at the Mashpee Wampanoag powwow.

Wampanoag Timeline

1500s

Wampanoag trade with European explorers.

1616-1618

Plague devastates many Wampanoag villages, including Patuxet.

1620

The Pilgrims land and establish Plymouth, a colony on the site of an abandoned village called Patuxet.

1621

- Samoset makes the first cont
between the Wampanoag an
the Pilgrims.
- Massasoit signs a peace treat
with the Pilgrims.
- Massasoit and 90 men join t
Pilgrims at Plymouth for a celebration of their harvest.

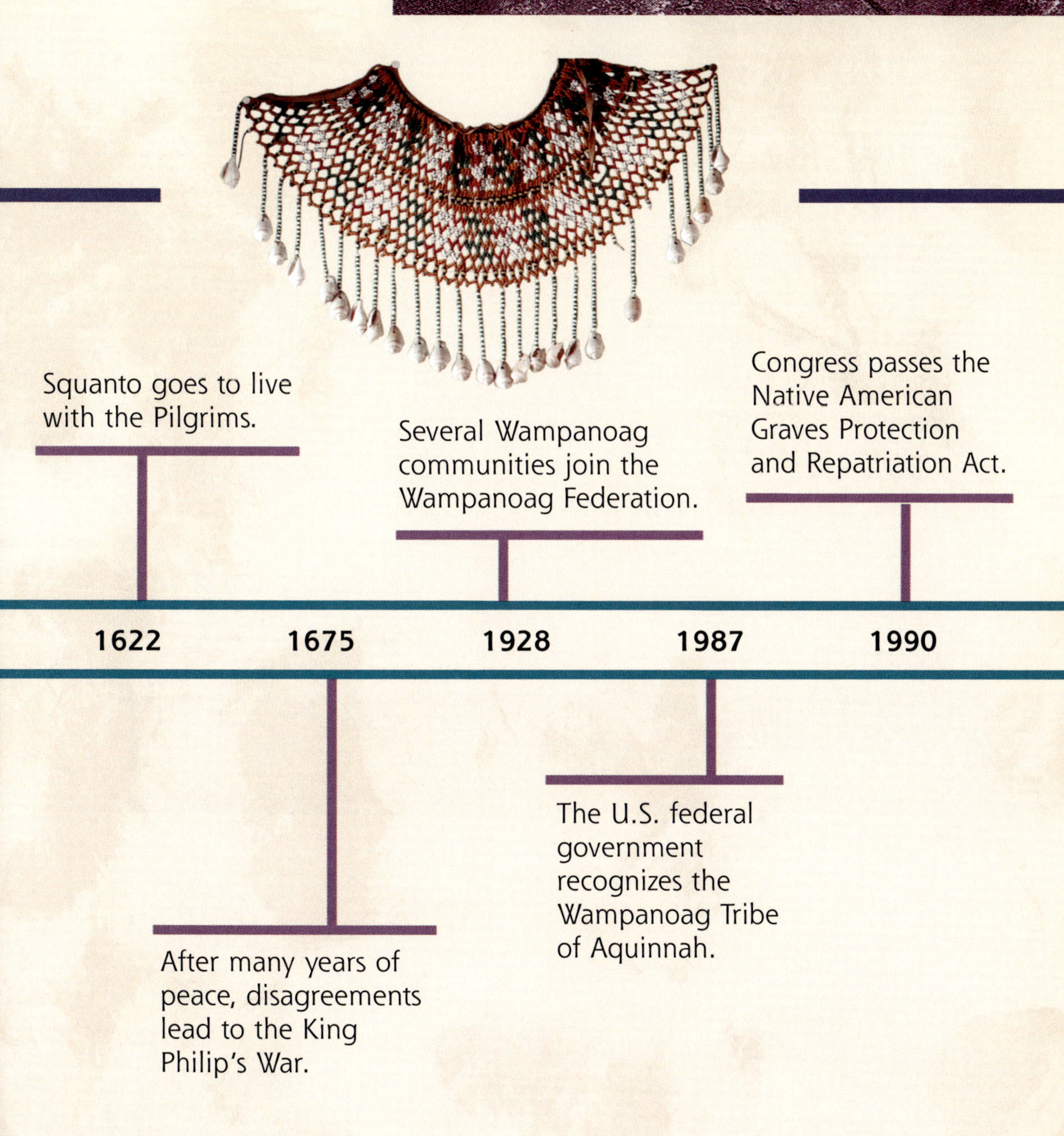

1622 — Squanto goes to live with the Pilgrims.

1675 — After many years of peace, disagreements lead to the King Philip's War.

1928 — Several Wampanoag communities join the Wampanoag Federation.

1987 — The U.S. federal government recognizes the Wampanoag Tribe of Aquinnah.

1990 — Congress passes the Native American Graves Protection and Repatriation Act.

Glossary

affirm (uh-FURM)—to agree with others that something is true

ancestor (AN-sess-tur)—a member of a person's family who lived a long time ago

epidemic (ep-uh-DEM-ik)—the rapid spreading of a disease

plague (PLAYG)—a disease that spreads rapidly and kills most of the people who catch it

preserve (pree-ZURV)—to protect something so it stays in its original form

sachem (SAY-chuhm)—leader or chief

sapling (SAP-ling)—a young tree

Internet Sites

Track down many sites about the Wampanoag.
Visit the FACT HOUND at *http://www.facthound.com*

IT IS EASY! IT IS FUN!

1) Go to *http://www.facthound.com*
2) Type in: 0736815686
3) Click on "FETCH IT" and FACT HOUND will find several links hand-picked by our editors.

Relax and let our pal FACT HOUND do the research for you!

Places to Write & Visit

Mashpee Wampanoag Tribal Council
P.O. Box 1048
Mashpee, MA 02649

Plimoth Plantation
P.O. Box 1620
Plymouth, MA 02362

Wampanoag Tribe of Gay Head (Aquinnah)
20 Black Brook Road
Aquinnah, MA 02535-1546

For Further Reading

Greene, Jacqueline Dembar. *Powwow: A Good Day to Dance.* A First Book. New York: Franklin Watts, 1998.

Lund, Bill. *The Wampanoag Indians.* Native Peoples. Mankato, Minn.: Bridgestone Books, 1998.

Manning, Helen. *Moshup's Footsteps: The Wampanoag Nation, Gay Head/Aquinnah.* Aquinnah, Mass.: Blue Cloud Across the Moon, 2001.

Peters, Russell M. *Clambake: A Wampanoag Tradition.* We Are Still Here. Minneapolis: Lerner, 1992.

Index

agriculture, 6, 8, 9, 10, 13, 21
Aquinnah Wampanoag, 6, 17, 18, 32, 37

children, 10, 13, 33, 36–37, 39
community, 6, 10, 13, 34, 42
cranberries, 17, 40, 42

Dermer, Thomas, 25
disease, 5–6, 22, 23, 26, 31

Easton, John, 30
elders, 10, 14, 19, 33, 39
Europeans, 9, 20, 21–22
    English, 25, 26, 28, 29, 30–31. See also Pilgrims

family, 10, 13, 14, 15, 16, 19, 27, 36, 42
fishing, 7, 10, 13, 16
food, 10, 13, 16, 17, 19, 22, 25, 26, 27, 40, 42

government, 6, 19, 34, 37

Hobbamock, 26
housing, 13–14
    neesquttow, 14, 15
    wetu, 13–14
hunting, 10, 13, 14–16, 21, 27

Indian Child Welfare Act, 36–37

King Philip. See Metacom
King Philip's War, 29, 30–31

Martha's Vineyard. See Noepe
Mashpee Wampanoag, 6, 35, 37, 42, 43
Massasoit, 24, 25, 26, 27, 28
Mayflower, 22
Metacom, 28, 30
Moshup, 18, 40
Moshup Pageant, 40

Narragansett Indians, 23
Native American Graves Protection and Repatriation Act, 34, 36
Noepe, 18, 32, 37

Patuxet, 6, 22, 25. See also Plymouth
Pilgrims, 6, 22–26, 27
Plimoth Plantation, 7, 42
Plymouth, 6, 7, 22, 24, 25, 26, 27, 28, 30, 42
powwow, 35, 42, 43

sachem, 19, 24, 25, 26, 27, 28, 34
Samoset, 25
slavery, 21, 25, 30, 31
socials, 42
spirituality, 16
Squanto, 25–26, 27

thanksgiving, 27, 40, 42
traditions, 6, 10, 16, 19, 22, 33, 37, 38, 39–40, 42
treaty, 23, 26, 28, 30

Wampanoag Nation, 6, 10, 19, 34, 42
Wamsutta, 28, 30